UNITED STATES ARMY UNIFORMS

1939-1945

Roy Dilley

ALMARK PUBLISHING CO. LTD., LONDON

First Published—June 1972

ISBN 0 85524 070 9 (hard cover edition)
ISBN 0 85524 071 7 (paper covered edition)

By the same author:
JAPANESE ARMY UNIFORMS AND EQUIPMENT, 1939-1945
SCALE MODEL SOLDIERS

Printed in Great Britain by
Vale Press Ltd., Mitcham, Surrey, CR4 4HR
for the publishers, Almark Publishing Co. Ltd.,
270 Burlington Road, New Malden,
Surrey, KT3 4NL, England

Introduction

MORE than 30 years have now elapsed since the United States of America entered World War 2, and details of the dress worn by American troops during that conflict have tended to become somewhat blurred. This book, whilst in no way claiming to be, as it were, a Quartermaster's catalogue of dress and equipment, provides for the student of military history and modeller alike, a sound working knowledge of American Army uniforms of the period. Items which were peculiar to the U.S. Army Air Force of that time have not been included, since they form the basis for a separate study of their own.

The term 'combat dress', as used in this work, refers to clothing worn by troops in training or in a theatre of operations, and is not confined to that worn specifically when in contact with the enemy. Thus mention is made for example, of alternative headgear to the steel-helmet, which although undoubtedly the prudent choice of the majority when in action or under fire, was usually replaced by something more comfortable in rear areas and out of action situations.

It should also be noted that 'olive drab', like British khaki, was a generic colloquial term covering many shades of colour from the brownish hue of winter service dress to the definite green of twill jungle uniforms. Constant washing and exposure to the elements under service conditions also affected to a greater or lesser degree the intensity of colour in a garment. It should be noted in passing, however, that there were several official 'olive drab' shades.

Emphasis has been placed on photographic illustrations, supported by detailed captions. All the photographs are from U.S. official sources, and have been chosen to show items of dress as issued, as well as actually being worn in the field. Much useful uniform data has been derived from official publications of the U.S. Quartermaster General's office.

Thanks are due to the Library staff at the Imperial War Museum, Lambeth, for their unfailing assistance, to Kenneth M. Jones and Peter Chamberlain for help with photographs and illustrations, and to the many American ex-soldiers who actually wore these uniforms and whose reminiscences have been of considerable value.

CONTENTS

ABOVE: A rifle squad firing on the enemy during the advance into Germany in 1945. They are using the M1 Garand rifle, and the two men on the right are in the act of reloading. All are wearing M1943 combat dress.

FRONT COVER: Infantry private in the two-piece jungle suit with mosquito face net, camouflage garnish in helmet, and camouflaged equipment. Note that camouflage greasepaint could also be applied to face and hands. The typical sleeve badges (formation signs) are those of Washington Military District (upper) and 82nd Airborne Division.
BACK COVER: Men of an infantry regiment based in England in the Spring of 1944 march past their regimental colours during an inspection by the divisional commanding general. They wear the olive drab service overcoat over the 1941 pattern service dress. Rifle they carry is the Garand M1.

1: Supply and Development

ALTHOUGH not entering World War 2 as a combatant until the end of 1941, the United States of America had for some time previous to this date been in a state of National Emergency, involving a considerable expansion of all its armed services, and a consequent increase in demand upon its resources both of men and material.

After 1918, the Quartermaster Corps of the U.S. Army had done some work to design clothing suitable for men fighting a modern war, but by and large the American soldier went into World War 2 clad in a uniform inherited from World War 1. Congress had, after that war, decided on economic grounds that it was unnecessary for the Army to have a dress uniform as such, and that such re-design as was felt to be required should be towards the development of combat clothing. However, as often happens with combat uniforms after a major conflict, that of the U.S. Army became gradually modified during the years of peace into the nearest thing to a dress uniform that was possible. Even so, it was not a real dress uniform, and as quickly became apparent after 1941, it was not a good combat uniform either. This was despite the modifications to the service coat made in the late 'thirties in an attempt to provide a more functional garment, and the design, in 1939, of a combat jacket to be used by troops in the field instead of the service coat.

Since the global nature of the war required troops to serve many types and extremes of climate from the Arctic to the tropics, the development of suitable garments for these conditions became urgent. Furthermore, the U.S. military authorities, observing the successes gained in combat by various special types of troops in the British and German armies, determined to organise similar formations in the U.S. service, making it necessary for the Quartermaster Corps to design, develop, and supply specialised clothing for ski, mountain, jungle, airborne, desert, armoured, and amphibious forces, and paratroops.

Initially the tendency was to produce specific types of garments for each of these troop categories, a situation which resulted in a large number of items, of which the functions overlapped in many cases. For example, the development of a short, wind-resistant parka for ski-troops clashed with a design for a similar but somewhat longer parka intended for use by snow-shoe patrols, and by several other specialised parkas. It soon became apparent that the administrative problems resulting from the production, storage, and distribution of so many specialised

Service Uniform of World War 1, 1917-1919: *The single breasted tunic with high collar and patch-pockets, and the breeches with cloth puttees wrapped round the legs from knee to ankle, was typical of uniforms worn by all the combatants during the latter part of the war. The British pattern steel helmet was adopted as standard by the U.S. Army at this time. A 'pudding basin' helmet based on the German 1915 pattern was designed by 1918, but was never issued. In slightly modified form it became the familiar M1 helmet of 1942.*

items was exercising a detrimental effect upon the efficiency of the supply system. A review of clothing stressed the fact that many garments had the same uses, and a study was undertaken in the summer of 1942 with the object of consolidating all items having the same function.

By the fall of the same year, the original trend towards the development of specialised clothing had been halted, and the emphasis from then on was placed on developing a standard basic combat dress for all arms and services. Only where conditions of climate or terrain made it absolutely imperative was specialised clothing designed, and even this was, where possible, made interchangeable with standard components of the basic uniform.

Of the many developments in military clothing which were now taking place, one of the most important was the adoption of the layering principle, together with the use of fabrics other than wool for the outer garments of combat dress. Applied in the first instance to Arctic dress, and later to all items of winter combat clothing, the layering principle provided the greatest degree of flexibility, that had yet been

Service Uniform of 1926: *This was very similar to the uniform of World War 1, except for an open step-collar, worn with collar and tie, and leather gaiters replacing the cloth puttees.*

achieved, enabling the wearer to adjust his basic combat wear by adding to or reducing the number of layers of clothing worn, according to the requirements dictated by the prevailing climatic conditions. Whilst aiming to develop clothing of a nature sufficiently flexible to be either warm or cool as circumstances demanded, the Quartermaster Corps was not able to provide any one outfit for a soldier that would give him the right degree of insulation whatever the temperature or the amount of his activity. Clearly, it is impossible to estimate, with any hope of accuracy, the nature of a soldier's activities in combat, since he may well find himself at one time in the midst of a swamp, and at another in a snug, dry barn. Similarly he may move from temperate farmland to windy hill-top or open mountainside all in the course of a single day, being too warmly clad in the morning, and without sufficient protection against the decrease in temperature by night. The layering principle went a long way towards solving the problem, but at the expense of adding somewhat to the total weight carried by each man.

In abandoning the concept of specialised clothing for special forces, and concentrating on the development of standard combat dress, the Quartermaster Corps emphasised the relationship of clothing to climate. In a man's adjustment to any given climate, clothing is the bridge between the two, and the finest garments are useless unless they are available in the correct places. A Climatic Research Unit was therefore set

Service Uniform by the late 1930s: *The jacket is the same as for the 1926 uniform, but trousers, worn with canvas leggings have taken the place of breeches.*

up within the Research and Development Branch, with the aim of arriving at a realistic basis for clothing distribution. This would replace the then accepted, but unrealistic principle which held that all areas between the Tropics of Cancer and Capricorn had a tropical climate, that all areas north of 56° north latitude and south of 56° south latitude were Arctic, and that all areas in between were temperate, without regard to the actual conditions prevailing. No less than 72 climatic zone maps were prepared by the Climatic Research Unit, with the purpose of allowing the rapid selection of appropriate clothing for any expedition to any part of the world at any season of the year. Eventually the Quartermaster Corps tables of basic allowances were revised to refer to four climatic zones, with boundaries slightly adjusted for ease of distribution. The principle on which the Military Planning Division was required to operate when relating clothing to climate was that maximum combat efficiency was possible if the clothing was ideal for the average conditions within a zone, but was also adequate under the worst conditions.

A considerable simplification of the overall Army Supply Program was achieved by the consolidation of garments having the same function into single types, and this trend was intensified in early 1944 by the commencement of an exercise to simplify even more the four-zone clothing items. Special emphasis was placed on the design of all-

The old and the new Service Uniforms, 1941: *Comparison between the two shows how the family characteristics were retained in the Service Coat during several minor design changes since 1918.*

purpose garments which could replace one or more standard items, and this trend towards simplification still dominated clothing development at the cessation of hostilities in 1945. A great deal of the work, it must be remembered had only been placed on a controlled, scientific basis as late as 1942, and had still to be completed when the War came to an end, but much data concerning military fabrics and garments had been accumulated by the Quartermaster Corps, with the valuable assistance of a number of university, private, and industrial laboratories.

ABOVE: The unwieldy campaign hat was still being used in 1941 but was soon discarded.

Side view of Service Coat, 1941, showing 'Bi-Swing' back. This feature was adapted from civilian sports coats, and was designed to allow the maximum freedom of action for the shoulders, in particular during drill movements as shown here.

9

Revised Service Coat, 1942: *With the adoption of a field jacket, the re-designed service coat became in effect a dress garment, and was worn as 'walking-out' dress and for occasions of a formal nature in camp and barracks, such as guard duty or parade. Note the slimmer fit and the elimination of the belt compared to picture on previous page.*

The make-up and characteristics of fabrics for military use had been studied exhaustively, together with the various finishes applied to them and the improvements in design and cut of garments which also helped to improve their combat performance.

However, the point must be made specifically that because the Quartermaster Corps, for various reasons was unready for the considerable demands that were made upon it by the outbreak of World War 2, it had of necessity to make rushed decisions, which caused frequent changes in specifications in the light of field experience. Initial lack of production capacity in the clothing industry, and shortages of the requisite materials also added to the multiplicity of specification revisions, making for difficulties, impatience, and irritation from the manufacturing point of view. Moreover, whilst the clothing industry, for the most part gave whole-hearted co-operation in the design and development of military clothing, its inherent conservatism often impeded the efficient working out of its problems with the help of research data.

It is convenient to group U.S. Army uniforms of the period under five main headings, namely: Service Dress; pre-1941 Combat Dress; 1941 Combat Dress; 1943 and 1945 Combat Dress; and specialised uniforms. However, one must bear in mind the fact that, because of supply and replacement factors, more than one of the above broad uniform types could be in service within the same unit simultaneously, whilst individual preference might lead a soldier to combine items from several types in his outfit at any given moment. It must also be appreciated that some of the more desirable items of specialised clothing were often 'acquired' and worn by troops other than those entitled to them as an official issue, but soldiers under combat conditions have a way of making themselves as comfortable as possible despite what may or may not be said in dress regulations!

In passing it is of interest to record that a proposal to change the army service dress from olive drab to slate grey colour was under favourable consideration by the War Department in 1940, experiments having shown that this colour offered better concealment value than olive drab However these plans were shelved when the massive expansion of the forces began since the upheaval necessary to put new uniform styles into production at that period would, of course, have been too considerable to contemplate. In the event such a colour change did not take place until some years after the war.

A military police post at a French cross-roads during the drive towards Coutances 1944. Note the helmet markings and brassards. All are wearing 1941 combat dress, and the soldier on the extreme left, not a military policeman, has 'acquired' a leather flying jacket.

2: Service Uniform

ALTHOUGH originally designed as an 'all purpose' outfit for wear in camps, garrisons, and in the field, the olive drab service uniform became the U.S. soldiers' dress wear, and after 1941 was used almost exclusively for formal occasions on duty, and for leaves and furloughs. It was felt under these circumstances to contribute greatly to the smartness of the men, and consequently to the maintenance of high morale. Worn with either the peaked service (garrison) cap, or the olive drab overseas cap piped with arm of service colour, it became to the civilian populations of the UK and Europe probably the most familiar of all American uniforms. This order of dress was worn with an olive drab flannel shirt. Until February 1942, a black neck-tie was worn. From this date on the tie was changed to olive drab.

In 1943 reports from operational zones in North Africa and Italy indicated that the service coat was of no value in forward areas, and its value in rear areas was limited due to the fact that it could only be satisfactorily cleaned by dry-cleaning, ie, it could not be washed. A recommendation was made to discontinue issue of the garment for overseas duty, but it was not until the fall of 1944 that the service coat was reclassified, in the European theatre of operations, as 'limited standard', and replaced as a standard item of issue by the olive drab

Coat style Olive Drab Flannel Shirt: *The shirt was normally worn, with or without a neck tie, under the field jacket in combat dress, or with the service coat. However under favourable climatic conditions on service, the field jacket was often removed and the shirt itself formed the principal upper garment.*

Summer Dress Uniform with peaked cap, 1942: *This uniform, of pale khaki cotton-twill, was the usual summer wear for 'walking out', and for duties in camp and barracks where fatigue dress was unsuitable. It could be worn with a neck tie, or with the collar open.*

wool field jacket. However, in the United States, the service uniform remained the standard winter 'dress' wear throughout the whole period of the war, with the khaki cotton, or later poplin, shirt and trousers, with the peaked service cap or khaki cotton overseas cap as standard summer dress wear.

OFFICERS' UNIFORMS

In general officers' uniforms were similar in style and function to those issued to enlisted personnel, particularly for combat and working garments. However the service coat and wool field jacket were usually privately purchased, and were superior in quality of material and cut. Both garments were used as 'dress' items, for 'walking out', and for formal and duty wear in camp and barracks. They were combined with trousers of the same material, or, by many officers, with special 'dress' trousers known as 'pinks', made from a warm pinkish beige superfine cloth.

Early in the War officers wore a brown leather 'Sam Browne' belt with the service coat, but this was soon replaced by a plain cloth belt of the same material as the coat, and fastened in front with a brass buckle.

Both the peaked garrison cap or the overseas cap were normal wear with service coat and wool field jacket, and frequently made their appearance in operational zones though usually as part of staff-officers' wear.

Officers' raincoats were of the belted trenchcoat type, with shoulder straps and a cape integral with the shoulders of the garment.

Summer Uniform, 1942: *These are the alternative ways of wearing the summer uniform, with the collar either open, or closed and with necktie. The headgear is the field cap trimmed with coloured piping to denote the arm of service of the wearer.*

BELOW: The full range of Army uniforms in 1941. From left is shown the old service dress with overcoat and the old campaign hat, the new service dress with peak cap, service dress with field jacket, mounted troops service dress with mackinaw, mounted troops summer dress with campaign hat, the new summer dress, dismounted troops summer dress with tropical helmet, armoured troops summer dress, twill suit, olive drab coveralls.

14

3: Combat Dress, 1939-1941

BETWEEN the proclamation of a state of emergency in 1939 and the outbreak of hostilities at the end of 1941, troops of the rapidly expanding ground forces wore combat clothing in the field at the great reception and training areas of the United States, and in overseas garrisons.

During the winter months the olive drab service coat and trousers, boots, gaiters and equipment were the usual wear, but from early 1941 the service coat was gradually replaced by the newly designed field jacket, made from olive drab water repellent cotton cloth, lined with warm flannel. Under severe winter conditions this would have been augmented by the overcoat, or the mackinaw, whilst really warm days would see the service coat or field jacket discarded as on page 16, which shows (in the lower picture) the standard summer combat dress.

In the tropics, and some American locations, the khaki cotton shirt and trousers, which were the standard service uniform, may also have been employed as combat dress, although olive drab twill suits took over in these areas in the field during 1941 for the most part.

The Olive Drab Field Jacket 1941: *Based broadly on the lines of a civilian windcheater, this jacket was made of wind-resistant, water-repellent cotton fabric, lined with shirting flannel. At first popular with the troops, its shortcomings were soon made apparent in operational theatres, and it became the subject of much adverse criticism, being superseded later in the war by the M1943 field jacket. The olive drab neck-tie dates this picture as post-February 1942.*

The Woollen Field Uniform for Dismounted Troops, 1941: *This shows the basic combat uniform, less helmet and equipment, that was worn by dismounted troops taking part in the initial American campaigns of World War 2, other than those in tropical and jungle areas. Compare with colour drawing opposite which shows the same uniform with the addition of steel helmet and equipment. Note the black tie and olive drab wool gloves.*

Combat headgear consisted, in addition to the old style helmet, of the wide-brimmed campaign hat, the neat little overseas cap, or a twill hat or cap worn with olive drab twill suits. A khaki cloth covered fibre sun-helmet was authorised in some tropical areas, and may have been worn under combat conditions, as may a lambskin lined winter cap.

The old and new Helmets. *On the left is the M1 helmet which in 1942 replaced the British Mk I helmet which the Americans had adopted in 1917. This demonstrates very clearly the superior design and shape of the new helmet, which was originally inspired by the German World War 1 helmet in 1918 when prototypes (wider and deeper) first appeared. The soldiers are wearing the 1941 form of combat dress with the field jacket omitted to reveal the flannel shirt as the outer garment. This was a summer practice in temperate climates. Note the bayonet frog and water bottle on opposite hips.*

LEFT: Private, Infantry, 1941. He is wearing the olive drab field jacket over the flannel shirt. 'Arm of service' badges are carried on the shirt collar and the neck-tie is black, Helmet is a blue/grey but could equally be olive drab.

RIGHT: Private, Military Police, 1944. He wears the basic 1941 combat dress with MP brassard and a 1st Army formation badge. The wool serge trousers were a 'brown' shade of olive drab with distinct blue tinge.

4: 1941 Combat Dress

MILITARY operations by U.S. forces early in 1942 were confined to tropical areas of the Pacific, and olive drab herringbone twill suits, both one and two-piece, were adopted for combat wear in the jungle conditions there encountered. Originally developed as fatigue clothing, these

Blue Denim Fatigue clothing 1940: *This was similar to the style of working clothing that had been used by the Army since before World War 1, except that a coat style had replaced the previous jumper pattern, (left below).*

One-piece Herringbone-Twill Suit for mechanics 1942: *The issue of this garment was restricted to mechanics and personnel of armoured units, and was olive drab in colour. Another 'new' item is shown here, a twill fatigue cap (right below).*

Two-piece Herringbone-Twill Fatigue Suit 1942: *This olive drab suit was the standard working fatigue clothing for all troops other than mechanics and armoured personnel. It replaced (in most units) the blue denim suits. Pending availability of specially designed jungle clothing, these garments were also used as the basis for combat dress in tropical climes, then being worn with helmets and personal equipment.*

cotton twill suits had, since the summer of 1941, gradually replaced the old blue denim working uniforms, and now also became accepted as summer combat dress, being used mainly in the Pacific areas.

By mid-1942 specially developed one and two-piece jungle suits had been standardised. Made from herringbone-twill printed with green camouflage patterns on one side and tan patterns on the other side of the cloth, these suits were reversible, and suitable for wear on open beaches as well as in the jungle. All buttons on closures and pocket flaps were concealed behind fly-fronts. It later became apparent under combat conditions that camouflaged suits, whilst satisfactory for snipers, in fact made their wearers more visible when in motion than did one colour garments, and studies were set in hand to develop more suitable jungle clothing.

In the European theatre of operations winter combat dress was worn throughout the year, the field jacket being discarded when conditions allowed.

The old style helmet was speedily replaced after the initial campaigns by the new pot-shaped M1 helmet worn over a pressed fibre liner, whilst herringbone-twill caps and hats, and knitted woollen caps and toques were other combat headgear. It is worthy of note that the helmet liner was frequently worn by itself as an out of action head-dress, even for formal purposes such as parades and guard duties.

Combat dress, based on service dress, as described in the previous chapter was the most common action clothing for American troops right

RIGHT: Private First Class of 3rd Infantry Division, winter 1944-1945, in M1943 combat dress with pile liner under field jacket and pile-lined winter issue boots. Wearing wool winter cap under helmet and wool gloves.

LEFT: Captain, Armored Forces, in one-piece twill combination suit and zip-front AFV field jacket.

LEFT: Private in two-piece camouflaged jungle suit with mosquito net and camouflaged equipment.

RIGHT: Technician (corporal) of 82nd Airborne Division, fighting order, June 1944. U.S. national flag emblem worn on right shoulder.

One-piece, Special, Herringbone-Twill Suit, 1943: *Herringbone-Twill material, although originally developed for fatigue clothing, became accepted as suitable for summer combat wear and for jungle garments as stated and illustrated on page 19. The design of the one-piece suit was changed to eliminate the cause of complaints by armoured force personnel of burns received from metal buttons coming into contact with the skin, and in this garment no metal actually touched the wearer. A stitched-in belt was incorporated and cuffs and trouser bottoms buttoned tight to protect against blast and gas. Because of its many buttons and gussets this garment was not generally popular.*

up to the war's end. This garb, distinguished instantly by the familiar canvas leggings and the short combat jacket has remained the best remembered clothing of the U.S. Army of the World War 2 period. It is popularly known as '1941 Combat Dress' mainly to distinguish it from the new M1943 Combat Dress (see next chapter), though, in fact, this was not an official designation. The enormous variation in the manner of wearing combat dress is seen in chapter 8, the pictorial section.

One-piece Jungle Suit, 1942:
A one-piece jungle suit for infantry and other fighting arms was specially requested by General McArthur in July 1942 after the early Bataan and Malaya campaigns. This was designed within a month and featured large external pockets, buttoned cuffs, a zippered front, and had internal braces or suspenders to take the weight of personal equipment worn with the suit. It was camouflaged green over a base colour, but was reversible with a plain tan colour inside for beach or open country combat.

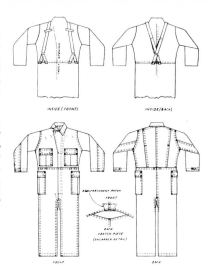

RIGHT: The fibre tropical helmet was an early casualty of the rationalisation scheme and was discarded early in 1942.

Two-piece camouflaged Herringbone-Twill Jungle Suit: *The one-piece jungle suit soon proved to have many disadvantages. It was insect proof while fully closed but the entire suit had to be opened for washing and natural functions, thus losing its value. When fully closed it was hot, and when wet it more than doubled its weight from 3lb to 7lb or over. This led almost immediately to the design of a two-piece suit with fly-front button openings but in the same camouflage pattern as the one-piece suit. This was standardised in May 1943. From this date on it replaced the one-piece suit which then became 'limited standard' until old stocks were used up. In March 1944 the two-piece suit was changed over from a camouflage pattern to a plain dark green (Olive Drab No. 7) as the camouflage pattern actually showed up on a moving man. Colour plate on page 21 shows the two-piece suit. OPPOSITE PAGE: The plain dark green two-piece suit shown in detail.*

Third Army

First Army

VIII Corps

Fourth Army

I Corps

IX Corps

1st Division

5th Division

6th Division

2nd Division

3rd Division

Typical formation badges; printed or embroidered cloth worn at left shoulder on combat and service dress.

29th Division

ABOVE, LEFT: **Mackinaw 1941:** *This was a cumbersome garment, originally designed for field wear in lieu of an overcoat. It was made of heavy canvas duck lined with woollen blanket material.*

ABOVE, RIGHT: **Modified Mackinaw 1942:** *In this item the weight of the outer fabric and of the lining was decreased in view of shortage of the original materials. Design of the collar was also incorporated so that it was made of the same material as the coat itself rather than the woollen fabric of the lining.*

Helmet Liner and complete assembly of M1 Helmet: *This new pot-shaped helmet worn with a fibre-liner had been developed to replace the British pattern helmet which had been standard since 1918. It owed much to the design of the German steel helmet of World War 1, and gave the wearer far better protection than did the former type.*

ABOVE, LEFT: **Revised Mackinaw 1943:** *Final version of the mackinaw, it no longer had a belt, and the collar had a notched lapel for easier buttoning. This was the garment that became known as the 'jeep-coat', and it was worn principally by transport personnel, to equip whom supplies of the M1943 field jacket were insufficient. A similar coat was issued to British Army personnel who referred to it as the jacket-reefer.*

ABOVE, RIGHT: **Melton Olive Drab Overcoat 1942:** *Although it had been expected that the overcoat would be an extremely useful item of combat clothing, in practice it was too clumsy, and was often discarded. The development of a winter combat uniform made the overcoat unnecessary as combat wear, and it became, in effect, a dress item.*

LEFT: **Woollen knitted Toque:** *The toque and a knitted 'stocking' cap were standard items of winter combat clothing.*

 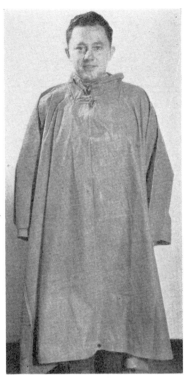

ABOVE, LEFT: **Enlisted Men's Raincoat:** *This design of raincoat was adopted in 1938, and with only minor modifications remained in service throughout World War 2. However, much thought and research development was given to the fabric from which it was made, and various types of waterproofing agents, rubber and synthetic resins were employed.*

ABOVE, RIGHT: **Synthetic Resin-Coated Poncho:** *Although simple in construction and versatile in use, this garment, a rectangle of cloth with a neck opening in the middle, was never really popular with the troops. Two or more could be fitted together to form a light bivouac type shelter. It was subsequently replaced by a lighter nylon version as described in the next chapter.*

Types of hats, 1941: *Some idea of the multiplicity of military headgear in service at the outbreak of the hostilities is given by this photograph. In fact the old British type steel helmet was also worn at this time during the opening campaigns in the Pacific Theatre. Included here are the old and new campaign hats, fatigue hat, garrison cap, and winter hat.*

5: 1943 and 1945 Combat Dress

THE experiences of troops in the field under combat conditions, and the strains being imposed upon supply and distribution organisations by the proliferation of specialised clothing items, led to the development of an all-purpose combat uniform which could be worn as outside garments for all seasons, and, utilising the layering principle, could be worn over woollen clothing and underwear for winter combat. This suit was comprised of the M1943 field jacket, made from wind and tear-resistant water-repellent cotton fabric, and trousers of the same material. It provided a battle suit for mild weather, and, when combined with pile fabric liners, gave adequate protection against severe winter conditions.

Testing of the new uniform was carried out in the U.S., and under combat conditions at Anzio, during the Italian Campaign, by personnel of the 3rd Division. Subsequently it was approved and requisitioned by issuing authorities in North Africa, but headquarters in the European Theatre of operations, held out against it until late 1944, owing to their preference for a uniform to resemble the British battledress suit, with which they had been very impressed. A newly designed olive drab cotton peaked field cap was worn with this outfit, and a hood for the field jacket was added in 1944.

New combat boots were also issued as part of the M1943 uniform, being made from leather with the flesh side turned out, and with wide cuffs at the top forming 'built-in' gaiters. Later, high-laced combat boots, similar to paratroopers' footwear, were introduced for all arms.

In the Pacific modifications to existing herringbone-twill garments continued, and by 1944 olive drab had replaced camouflaged patterns almost entirely. Constant work was carried out to develop a really satisfactory jungle suit, and designs were tested under active service conditions throughout 1944 and 1945, but it was not until the summer of 1945 that the new lightweight poplin jungle uniform was approved. Two piece suits had proved to be far more popular with the troops than one piece garments, which had the grave disadvantage, since no drop seat was incorporated, of requiring a man virtually to strip naked whenever he needed to attend to a major call of nature, thus exposing himself to every hazard of insects and environment! The two piece M1945 Lightweight Jungle Suit was virtually the tropical equivalent of the M1943 Combat Suit and was superficially similar though much simpler in cut and, of course, made of entirely different material. The 41st Infantry Division on Biak Island was issued with the new suit for tests in September 1944, and later other units in the Pacific and South East Asia were issued with it. The suit was standardised in July 1945 and was issued soon after.

501st (Parachute) Infantry Regiment

88th Division

99th Division

2nd Army

45th Division

101st (Airborne) Division

4th Armored Division

Washington Military District

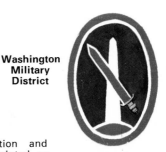

Typical formation and unit badges; printed or embroidered cloth.

Worn at left shoulder on combat and service dress.

AA Command, Western Command

82nd (Airborne) Division

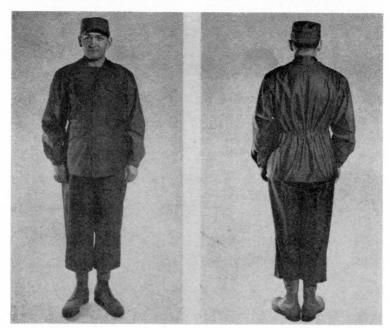

M1943 Combat Dress: *This represents a considerable advance in design over the earlier forms of combat dress. The basic suit, with cap, is shown.*

Both the M1943 Combat Suit and the M1945 Lightweight Jungle Suit were major landmarks in the history of military uniform development. They embodied all the lessons from several years of combat experience, and most military forces in the Western world have since 1945 adopted similar types of combat uniform, including the British. The M1943 field jacket was considered by some experts to be the best and most functional item of combat attire developed during World War 2. Early M1943 suits were made with a sateen outer layer (the inner layer was poplin) which gave a characteristic smooth finish with a slight sheen. In 1945 Oxford cloth was substituted for the sateen as an economy measure; this was coarse and more matt in appearance.

The other combat dress of this period was the M1944 Wool Field Jacket a garment restricted in issue to Europe and North Africa—though it could be worn elsewhere by soldiers who had been issued with it. This garment was a copy of British battledress though made in finer material and with a slimmer cut. In 1943 the Commander, ETO, authorised orders for local manufacture in England, and in November 1944 the jacket was officially standardised by the U.S. Army. Like British battledress, the wool field jacket was intended for both combat and parade wear and it could be worn under the M1943 combat jacket in winter. In practice, however, it was more often kept carefully pressed for parade or walking-out wear. When issued it replaced the wool serge service jacket.

In combat the dress of officers was identical with that of their men, only their rank badges serving to distinguish them at close quarters,

LEFT: In 1944 a hood, which could be worn over other types of head-gear, was added to the M1943 field jacket. It fastened to the top button and shoulder-loop buttons of the jacket, and could also be fitted to the officer's trench coat. RIGHT: The M1943 field jacket had an adjustable drawstring waist. Note the M1944 wool field jacket worn underneath, though this garment was rarely so worn. The M1943 field cap is also shown.

RIGHT: The Pile Jacket Liner worn with the M1943 field jacket to offer adequate protection against severe weather conditions in winter or cold zones.

since items such as pistol holsters, bino-cular and map cases, etc, were also part of the equipment of certain non-commis-sioned officers and men.

Cuff stripes and insignia

General
(top coat
only)

Officer
(service
coat)

Warrant Officer
(overcoat
only)

Enlisted Men
(indicating commissioned
service in World War 1.
not worn by others)

Formation badge

Rank badges

Enlisted Man's
sleeve badges

Wound
stripes

1917-18 service stripes
(above) and 1942-45
service strips (below).

General Staff Corps (Army HQ)

Military Police

Fire Company

Typical brassards

Officers' lapels
with branch of
service badge (infantry)

*Drawings are
not to common
scale.*

Enlisted Man's lapel
with unit badge as worn
by some special units or
distinguished regiments.

LEFT: Utilisation of the layering principle in M1943 Combat Dress is here demonstrated by a soldier wearing the M1943 field jacket with beneath it several layers of warm clothing, ie, woollen underwear, flannel shirt, high neck sweater, and pile jacket liner.

RIGHT: M1943 Combat Dress shown in cold weather with neck fastened, and back flap of M1943 field cap folded down. Note gloves for cold weather.

Wool Field Jacket 1944: *Originally designed on the lines of the British battle-dress blouse, this jacket was intended to replace the service coat as a field garment which could also be used as a dress item. In practice, troops in the field seldom employed it in combat dress, preferring to reserve it solely for dress purposes on leaves and furloughs. Its issue was restricted to the European and North African Theatres, but troops returning to the U.S.A. were authorised to wear it in lieu of the service coat.*

Two-piece Special Lightweight Jungle Suit, 1945: *In this suit a light poplin fabric had replaced the herringbone-twill, and a loose fitting coat had been adopted. Compare with earlier jungle suits shown in the previous chapter.*

BELOW: A high neck sweater (shown with buttons fastened) was another important component part in the layering principle, supplementing the pile liner. It was dark olive drab.

ABOVE: Experimental battle dress in North African Theatre 1943. As part of the development of the M1943 field-jacket, several sample garments were sent to various service boards for testing, and a few were also sent to the North African theatre of operations where they were received favourably, although recommendations were made for certain features to be changed.

Field Cap M1943 and Pile Cap: The programme of standardisation of items having the same use resulted in the all-purpose field cap M1943 (shown with back flap lowered) and the cold-climate pile-cap which replaced no less than three similar winter issue items.

Lightweight Poncho: *Nylon fabric was utilised for this item, which was standardised in 1944 as a replacement for the earlier synthetic poncho. It could be used as a raincoat, individual shelter, sleeping bag, or with several others to form a tent. It had a drawstring neck opening and double snap-fasteners down the sides. It can be seen below in use as a sleeping bag.*

6: Specialised Clothing

AS has already been stated, the raising of specialised troop formations, with their consequent demands for clothing suited to their particular functions, resulted in the development of a multiplicity of items, each with its own supply and distribution problems. Most of these designs were manufactured in relatively small quantities, and had a limited issue, eventually becoming superseded as the rationalisation policy took effect. However, armoured personnel and airborne/paratroopers retained certain distinctive items, which were of course manufactured on a much larger scale.

Men of the armoured forces had a one-piece twill suit, and a field jacket of twill with a pile fabric lining, knitted woollen collar, cuffs, and waist band, which was fastened in front by a long zip fastener from hem to collar. Special composition helmets were issued to shield their heads from accidental damage in their vehicles, but this headgear was often discarded in favour of the standard issue steel helmets and liners, which gave better protection against the efforts of the enemy to inflict intentional injury!

BELOW, LEFT: An excellent view of the one-piece twill tank suit, with the hood attached to the neck and shoulders, worn with a special leather tank helmet. BELOW, RIGHT: The one-piece tank suit worn with the zip-front field jacket. Man beyond is wearing the enlisted men's raincoat. The M1911 pistol is carried.

A close view of the composition protective helmet for armour personnel. Note the goggles. The men are in the one-piece twill tank suit.

For airborne/paratroops, a twill field jacket was adopted, having slanting breast pockets and reinforced elbows. This was worn with trousers of the same material, which featured capacious hip-pockets and reinforcement at the knees. Black leather boots of a high-laced type giving maximum support to the ankles, and, often, a camouflaged neck cloth completed the ensemble.

Special combat boots with rubber soles and uppers fastened by metal clips, and leather boots with pile fabric linings were developed for use in extremes of wet, mud, and cold, whilst troops fighting in jungle areas were issued with high-laced, rubber-soled canvas boots.

It must be stressed again that clothing items supplied to specialist formations frequently found their way, by one means or another, into the possession of troops for whom they were not standard issue, but in most cases, under active service conditions, a blind eye was turned by the authorities on most irregularities of dress.

U.S. troops in white camouflage clothing patrol the Domanial Forest, January 1945. This is an example of extemporised special garments, the shrouds being made at unit level from white sheeting. There were several variations.

Complete regulation dress for airborne troops. Note slanting breast pockets in jacket, reinforced trouser knees, and high-laced boots. The paratroop dress was in light olive drab and washed out to give a greyish neutral colour. This NCO is a technical sergeant.

Dressed in white snow suits, these U.S. medical corpsmen attend to a 'casualty' during a demonstration at Ettlebruck, Luxembourg, January 1945. This special winter suit was introduced in the winter of 1944-45. It was in short supply at first.

BELOW: Blending nicely into the leafy background, this soldier is wearing the camouflaged jungle suit and other accessories specially developed for warfare in the Pacific Area. Note the camouflaged helmet, the anti-mosquito mask and gloves, and the canvas and rubber boots. The band on the helmet is for affixing local foliage.

LEFT: A relatively rare item of clothing was the officers' top coat which saw only limited issue and appeared to go mainly to senior officers, and generals. It was similar to the 'British Warm' but of looser cut, beige in colour. It could be seen with or without the belt, and, as worn here by General Eisenhower, had generals' cuff lace and epaulette rank badges.

RIGHT: Senior officers in the European Theatre of operations wore a stylised version of the olive drab wool field jacket, with slit pockets, narrow waist band, and faced revers. Officers' cuff lace and other corresponding insignia from the service jacket were worn. The standard M1944 wool field jacket was also worn by senior officers and General Eisenhower, for example, was photographed in both styles. In this picture the general talks to a private in summer service dress, wearing serge trousers and the olive drab flannel shirt. Note the bayonet holder on the haversack.

7: Badges and Insignia

THE style and system of rank insignia and arm of service distinctions was admirably simple and logical in the United States Army. Officers' and Warrant Officers' badges of rank in metal or embroidery were worn on each shoulder-strap of the service coat, field jacket, raincoat, over-coat, and on each shoulder of working clothing where no shoulder straps were provided. When the olive drab or khaki shirt was worn without the service coat or any of the above outer garments, badges of rank were worn on the right side of the collar, except for generals of the line, who wore rank badges on both sides of the collar. Ranks were frequently indicated on the front of the steel helmet, by means of painted emblems, or by pinning a metal shoulder badge to the helmet cover if worn, and also on the left side of the garrison cap, about $1\frac{1}{2}$ inches from the front. The garrison cap was piped around its edges with cords which were

OFFICERS' RANK BADGES

All silver coloured, metal except where otherwise marked; warrant officers' badges introduced January 1942.

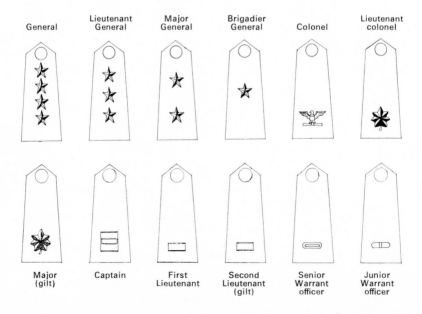

| General | Lieutenant General | Major General | Brigadier General | Colonel | Lieutenant colonel |

| Major (gilt) | Captain | First Lieutenant | Second Lieutenant (gilt) | Senior Warrant officer | Junior Warrant officer |

ENLISTED MEN'S RANK BADGES

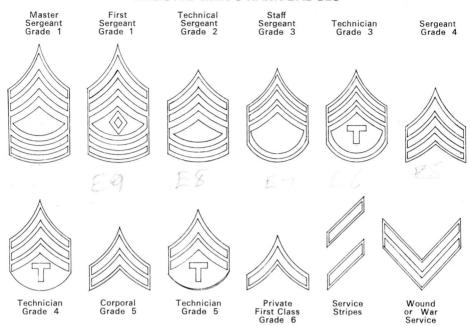

| Master Sergeant Grade 1 | First Sergeant Grade 1 | Technical Sergeant Grade 2 | Staff Sergeant Grade 3 | Technician Grade 3 | Sergeant Grade 4 |

| Technician Grade 4 | Corporal Grade 5 | Technician Grade 5 | Private First Class Grade 6 | Service Stripes | Wound or War Service |

Notes: Rank chevrons were olive drab on blue-grey background; service stripes were the same for regular service but olive drab on a yellow background for National Guard service; wound or war service (1917-19) stripes were gold. The technician class was established in January 1942.

coloured gold for generals, gold and black for other commissioned officers and silver and black for warrant officers.

The ranks of enlisted men were shown by olive drab chevrons on a blue-grey background, and were worn on both sleeves of the service coat, field jacket, overcoat, working clothing, and shirt where this was worn without any of the preceding outer garments. Some NCOs also indicated their ranks on the front of their steel-helmets with painted or metal emblems.

Insignia of Arm of Service were worn in addition to badges of rank in certain orders of dress. On the peaked garrison cap, officers and enlisted men wore the arms of the United States, the former in cut-out form, and the latter superimposed on a brass disc—later replaced by a badge in olive drab plastic. Warrant officers wore a badge distinctive to their rank. On the overseas cap, officers and warrant officers carried their badges of rank, as noted above, but enlisted personnel displayed their arm or service insignia, and the edges of their caps were piped in a distinctive arm of service colour (see separate table). Officers wore a cut-out metal 'U.S.' on both ends of the collar of the service coat, and, centred under the 'U.S.' on both lapels, arm of service insignia, which was also carried on the left side of the collar of the olive drab or khaki

ENLISTED MEN'S ARM OF SERVICE BADGES

Collar
badge

Collar
badge
(with unit
number-pre
1940)

Armored
Forces
(from
1940)

Cavalry
(until
1940)

Engineer
Corps

Field
Artillery

Infantry

Medical
Corps

Military
Police

Ordnance
Department

Quartermaster
Corps

Signal
Corps

Tank
Destroyer
Forces

Special
Service
Force

Notes: Originally 1 inch gilt discs, later olive drab plastic; 'U.S.' worn on right lapel, arm of service badge on left lapel; 'U.S.' worn on both lapels by unattached men or trainees. Not shown here are ROTC (reserve officer candidates—torch of learning), detached list (U.S. arms), Transportation Corps (winged wheel), Coast Artillery (crossed guns and shell), Mine Planter Service (crossed guns, shell and mine), Finance Department (lozenge), Chemical Warfare Troops (same as officer's design—opposite page).

shirt when the coat was not worn. Warrant officers also had the cut-out 'U.S.' on their collars, but used the Warrant officer's distinctive badge as insignia of arm or service. For enlisted men the 'U.S.' was super-imposed on a 1 inch disc of bronze or brass, later olive drab plastic, and was worn on the right collar end of the service coat, with the arm or service insignia on a similar disc in a corresponding position on the left. Distinctive insignia were worn on both lapels of the enlisted men's service coat, and in some cases on officer's shoulder straps. Both sleeves of the officer's service coat carried a half-inch band of olive drab braid midway between the cuff and the elbow, whilst in the same position on the sleeves of warrant officers and enlisted men who had served as commissioned officers in World War 1 there was a $\frac{1}{2}$ inch band of forest green braid.

Wound and War Service chevrons, both types referring to service in World War 1, were worn on the service coat by officers, warrant officers, and enlisted men, the former with point downwards on the lower half of the right sleeve, and the latter in a similar position on the left sleeve. The chevrons were awarded for 6 months service in the zone of advance, with an additional chevron for each 6 months of similar service thereafter, and were gold in colour. Where a chevron was awarded for less than 6 months service in the zone of advance, it was coloured sky blue.

Stripes for service other than that in World War 1, were of olive drab on a blue grey background, or a buff background for National Guard

OFFICERS' ARM OF SERVICE BADGES

Collar badge
(both lapels)

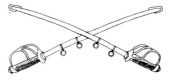

Cavalry

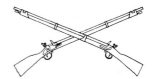

Infantry

Note: Other branches not shown
had same devices as illustrated
opposite.

Military Police

Chemical Warfare
(mauve rhomboid)

Ordnance Dept

Quartermaster
Corps (blue wheel rim)

Tank Destroyer
Forces

Transportation
Corps

Medical Corps

Medical Corps
(Administration)

Signal Corps
(white/red centre left, and
red/white centre, right flags)

General Staff Corps
(grey star, red/white/
blue device)

Chaplain—Christian
(silver)

Chaplain—Jewish
(silver)

Above: Warrant officer's cap badge.

Right: Enlisted Man's cap badge (on disc). Officer's cap badge similar but in cut-out form.

service. They were awarded for a continuous period of three years honourable service, with another stripe for each additional period of three years service. These stripes were worn only by enlisted men, and were displayed on the lower part of the left sleeve, at an angle of 45°, the lower end to the front.

No wound chevrons were authorised for World War 2, the Purple Heart decoration being awarded in lieu, the ribbon of which was worn on the left breast of the service coat above the pocket.

Buttons on the service coat both for officers and enlisted men were originally of gilt, later bronze, coloured metal and carried the embossed arms of the United States, except for Engineer Corps officers, who had a special device, showing an eagle flying over a bastion with embrasures surrounded by water, and carrying in its beak a scroll with the word 'Essayons'.

Shoulder Sleeve Insignia

Shoulder sleeve insignia were coloured cloth patches, usually with some kind of numerical, geometric or heraldic device superimposed upon them generally in bright colours, and were worn on the left sleeve just below the shoulder. They served to identify the wearer's army corps, or division, and in a few cases, regiment, and had obvious advantages in the building up of 'esprit de corps' and in aiding recognition and re-assembly of troops during and after action, though they were not always worn in combat. All these devices had to be approved by the War Department, and were for the most part kept as simple as possible, and consistent with the laws of heraldry. An interesting feature was that where heads or faces were included in a design they were either re-presented as 'full-face' or facing to the front of the wearer. A selection of shoulder sleeve insignia is shown on pages 24 and 29.

American troops being inspected by Major General Russell P. Hartle in March 1942 at Londonderry, Northern Ireland. These were the first American soldiers to arrive in Europe and they wear the standard pre-war winter service dress with British Mk I steel helmet. Note the black ties, later changed for olive drab, and the web equipment and haversack worn in marching order. NCO's at right have whistles. The company commander wears infantry arm of service badges on his lapels while the staff officer behind him has General Staff Corps badges. Officers' braid is seen on the sleeves and tan and brown leather gloves are in evidence.

Arm Bands or Brassards

In addition to the identification marks discribed above, certain soldiers (sometimes) wore arm bands or brassards to show the particular type of work they were doing. These brassards were worn on the left sleeve (attached permanently) midway between the elbow and the shoulder and were as follows:

(1) General Staff Corps—the letters 'GSC' in rounded black type were placed in the centre of the brassard. The colours for the various headquarters were as follows:

    (a) Divisions—Red with white letters.

    (b) Army Corps and Corps areas—blue and white, blue uppermost, with red letters.

    (c) Armies—white and red, white uppermost, with blue letters.

(d) HQs of field forces and War Dept—blue, white and red in order from top to bottom with blue letters.

(2) Military Police—the letters 'MP' in block type in white on a dark blue background.

(3) All persons in the Military Service rendered neutral by the terms of the Geneva Convention in time of war—a red Geneva cross on a white background.

(4) Men on Recruiting duty—the words 'Recruiting Service' in white block letters on a dark blue background.

(5) Members of Fire Truck and Hose Companies—the word 'Fire' in white block letters on a red background.

(6) Port Officers—the letters 'ATS' in black, followed immediately below by designation of position of department, on a buff background.

(7) Members of Veterinary Service — a green cross on a white background.

(8) Newspaper correspondents, photographers, and broadcasters attached to and authorised to accompany forces of the Army of the U.S. in the theatre of operations:

(a) Journalists, Feature Writers and Radio Commentators—a white block letter 'C' 2 inches high on green background.

(b) Photographers—a white block letter 'P' 2 inches high on a green background.

(9) Technical Observers and Service Specialists accompanying U.S. Army Forces in the field—the letters 'T.O.' in black 1¼ inches in height on an orange background.

Branch and Arm of Service Colours

Official Colours of Branches and Agencies, used as coloured cords on campaign hats, and as piping on overseas caps:

Branch	Colour
Adjutant-General's Corps	Dark blue, piped with scarlet.
Armour	Yellow (green, piped with yellow, 1943).
Artillery	Scarlet.
Chaplains	Black.
Chemical Corps	Cobalt-blue, piped yellow.
Cavalry	Yellow.
Coastal Artillery Corps	Scarlet.
Corps of Engineers	Scarlet, piped white.
Detached enlisted men's list	Green.
Field Artillery	Scarlet.
Finance Dept.	Silver grey, piped with golden yellow.
General Staff Corps	Gold, piped with black.
Inactive Reserve	Brown, piped with white.
Infantry	Light blue.
Inspector General's Dept	Dark blue, piped with light blue.
Judge Advocate Gen's Dept	Dark blue, piped with white.
Medical Dept	Maroon, piped with white.
Military Intelligence Reserve	Golden yellow, piped with purple.
Military Police	Yellow, piped with green.

Though not covered specifically in this book the Army Air Corps was an army branch and wore army uniforms for everyday duties. Here Lieutenant General Lewis H. Brereton (left) and his deputy, Major General Ralph Royce (9th U.S. Air Force), show typical service dress. General Brereton is in service dress with cap and General Royce is in the optional 'pinks' and wears a garrison cap. The military policemen are in full parade dress, with service uniform, brassards and belts. Note 9th Air Force sleeve badges (formation signs) and two styles of MP cap covers.

Branch	Colour
National Guard Bureau	Dark blue.
Ordnance Dept Corps	Crimson, piped with yellow.
Permanent Professors of U.S. Military Academy	Scarlet, piped with silver grey.
Quartermaster's Corps	Buff.
Signal Corps	Orange, piped with white.
Specialist Reserve	Brown, piped with golden yellow.
Warrant Officers	Brown.
Tank Destroyer Forces	Black.
Transportation Corps	Brick red, piped with golden yellow.
Women's Army Corps	Old gold, piped with moss-tone green.

49

RIGHT: General Lee in parade dress in 1944 wears a Sam Browne belt and 'pinks'. He has tan gloves and wears on his sleeve a formation sign, three World War 1 service stripes, and officer's cuff braid.

LEFT: Contrast in general's service dress, Europe, 1944. From left to right are Major General James M. Gavin with helmet, belt, and high boots, General Eisenhower in M1944 olive drab field jacket (ie, 'battle-dress'), General Ridgeway in olive drab field jacket, garrison cap, and high boots, and General Brereton in the officers' style blouse and service cap. Note variation in shades of olive drab cloth.

8: Uniforms in Service

PREVIOUS chapters have shown the various regulation dress items in wear during the years 1940-45. As was pointed out earlier, however, the quick succession of uniform development in this period meant that there was a wide variation in orders of dress seen at any one time. In addition there were personal dress adaptations in the interest of comfort. This section shows typical service scenes wherein are shown all types of dress as they actually appeared in everyday wear. The reader can make a ready comparison with the official dress pictures on previous pages.

Infantry and an M10 tank destroyer unit advancing into the Paris suburbs, August 1944. Note the varying styles of wearing the trousers over the canvas leggings, and the discarded combat jackets tucked through their belts. M1941 Combat Dress.

Infantryman in 1941 combat dress near Angers, August 1944. On his back he carries the basic man-pack frame, with an entrenching tool stuck through the straps.

Infantry in 1941 combat dress pass a knocked-out Tiger tank in July 1944. Each soldier has worked out his own set of equipment, and the man of the extreme left carries a radio on his back.

LEFT:
The Commanding General of the U.S. 45th Division checks his map with one of his regimental commanders, a lieutenant-colonel. Both are in variations of M1941 combat dress, but the general has paratrooper's boots. and the colonel wears M1943 type anklets. Note the methods of wearing rank badges, on helmets, shirt collars, and shoulders of combat jacket.
BELOW:
Details of the M1941 combat dress are well revealed in this study of troops operating a field telephone.

A column of infantry and transport advancing towards St Lo, July 1944. The soldiers are wearing 1941 combat dress, with variation of equipment components. Note that the two men on the rear off-side of the jeep are wearing their entrenching tools on opposite hips, proving how illogical it is to adopt a dogmatic attitude towards what was or was not worn at any given point of time.

The first American jeep to cross the German frontier, at Roelgen in September 1944. The crew are wearing the then newly issued M1943 combat dress.

Soldiers of the U.S. 7th Army at Guiderkirch in March 1945. They are wearing a mixture of 1941 and M1943 combat dress (three seated). The officers on the right can be distinguished by the rank badges on the front of their helmets.

Rear view of troops in M1943 combat dress in the Meurthe Valley, November 1944. Note the variety of equipment.

Artillery crews of 7th Army in November 1944, wearing M1943 combat dress, without equipment.

A good example of variety in dress is provided by this jeep-load of U.S. soldiers in the Moselle area of France. The standing soldier wears his overcoat, the sergeant is in M1943 combat dress, and the man on the bonnet front is wearing 1941 combat dress and has a cover on his helmet.

ABOVE: Close-up of the M1943 combat jacket is afforded by these machine-gunners at Rimbingen, January 1945. The pile liner is just visible inside the jacket of the nearest man. The gun is the Browning ·30 M1917A1 machine gun. BELOW: Rear view of M1943 combat dress worn by infantrymen marching through Keffenach, December 1944. Note the hoods buttoned on the necks of combat jackets, but thrown back; also folded poncho on right hip of nearest soldier.

Infantry of U.S. 7th Army, near Raon L'Etape, November 1944. They wear M1943 combat dress, but man third right is in the armoured troops' zippered field jacket. Two leading men are junior officers.

U.S. Paratroopers in Normandy. Points to note are the different styles of helmet netting, the camouflaged neck cloths, national flag on right shoulders, gloves, and high-laced boots. The left hand man wears a pistol in a shoulder holster.

Officer of airborne forces. Note his armament, a rifle, a ·45 cal automatic pistol, and grenades, with two ammunition bandoliers.

U.S. Paratroops in a French village on 'D' day, 6th June, 1944. Note the airborne type equipment and variety of armament, knives, etc.

Two paratroop officers, having been captured by the Germans, rejoice in style on their release by other U.S. Airborne forces. Note particularly the U.S. national flag on right shoulder, with divisional sign on left shoulder (obliterated by censor). Also high-laced boots and camouflaged neck cloths.

OPPOSITE PAGE: Wearing the one-piece green twill jungle suit, this U.S. soldier is involved in action on the island of Guadalcanal in the South Pacific. Notice the 'dog-tag' identity discs on a string around his neck, and the trouser bottoms worn loose over the canvas gaiters.

M1945 jungle combat dress worn by troops invading Tokashiki Island, March 1945. (U.S. Navy).

An example of ponchos in use, by troops on Okinawa in May, 1945,
listening in on their radio to the news of victory in Europe. The picture
also shows very well the two-part nature of the American steel helmets,
ie, the fibre liner worn beneath the helmet proper. Note local tactical
symbol (77th Division) in white on helmet.

In this picture of a ·50 calibre anti-aircraft machine gun crew two variants
of the green twill jungle suit are depicted. The soldier wielding the pick-
axe is wearing the one-piece version, whilst his comrade with the spade
has the two piece suit together with the new style jungle hat.

Here the one-piece green twill jungle suit is worn by soldiers clearing a Japanese bunker on Luzon island in the Phillipines in January, 1945.

U.S. troops in Burma, January 1945, crossing a pontoon bridge at Kazu, some thirty miles from the Irrawaddy river. They are dressed in the one-piece green twill jungle suit, and the second man in the file is wearing British type wrap around cloth puttees.

An anti-aircraft gun crew wearing only olive drab shorts in the heat of India, March 1944. Their weapon is a water-cooled ·50 calibre machine gun.

Here the two-piece camouflaged jungle suit is being worn in France, where it was specially issued to some infantry units in the wooded areas of the Brest Peninsula, June 1944. Note the entrenching tools carried from the waist belt.

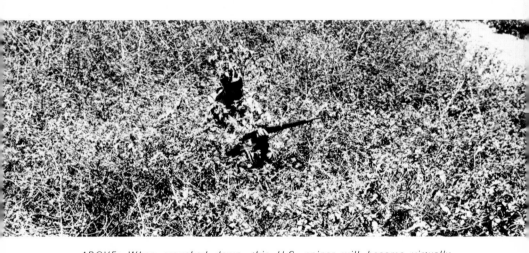

ABOVE: When crouched down, this U.S. sniper will become virtually invisible in his camouflaged jungle suit among the heavy vegetation of a Southwest Pacific Island.

OPPOSITE PAGE: Equipped against all the likely hazards of jungle fighting this soldier in the Southwest Pacific Area is wearing the poncho over the camouflaged jungle suit. The mosquito-mask, and high laced rubber and canvas boots were specialised items designed for this type of campaign.

ABOVE: The crew of this 75 mm gun motor carriage M3 are wearing the 1941 twill summer combat dress, with full equipment. BELOW: Infantry in the same dress order at Gafsa, Tunis, 1943.

Crewmen in one-piece twill tank suits, carrying ammunition to their M4A3 medium tank, which is surrounded by floodwater in Eastern France. Note the use of the steel helmet rather than the protective tank helmet.

The typical infantryman of 1944-45 is portrayed by this bazooka team wearing M1943 combat dress. The left hand man has the canvas leggings of 1941 type, and the other soldier wears pile-lined winter issue boots. The olive drab scarf was official issue. Compare with the 1942 infantrymen shown on page 47.

9: Infantry Weapons

THOUGH this book is not specifically about weapons and cannot cover them in detail, some basic data concerning personal arms and infantry weapons is given here, mainly to help the reader with a quick identification of the weapons shown in most 'action' photographs.

Pistol, Automatic, Calibre ·45, M1911A1, M1911

Calibre:	*·45, M1911 cartridge, ball ammunition.*
Magazine:	*Box type, single line. Capacity 7 cartridges (1 in breech = 8 for capacity of pistol).*
Muzzle velocity:	*810 ft/s.*
Weight of bullet:	*230 grains, lead with metal jacket.*
Striking energy:	*340 ft lbf.*
Barrel length:	*5 in.*
Overall length:	*8½ in.*
Weight:	*39 oz.*
Accurate range:	*75 yd.*
Maximum range:	*1,600 yd approx.*
Operation by recoil.	

See page 40 for photograph.

Pistol, Smith and Wesson ·45, 1917 Revolver

Calibre:	*·45, M1911 cartridge with clips.*
Cylinder:	*6 chambers.*
Muzzle velocity:	*810 ft/s.*
Weight of bullet:	*230 grains, lead with metal jacket.*
Striking energy:	*340 ft lbf.*
Barrel length:	*5½ in.*
Overall length:	*10¾ in.*
Weight:	*36¼ oz.*
Accurate range:	*75 yd.*
Maximum range:	*1,600 yd approx.*

Pistol, Colt ·45 1917 Revolver

Calibre:	*·45, M1911 cartridge with half moon clips.*
Cylinder:	*6 chambers.*
Ballistics as for automatic pistol.	
Barrel length:	*5½ in.*
Overall length:	*10¾ in.*
Weight:	*40 oz.*

Two views of the ·30, ·06 Springfield 1903 rifle, showing the rear sights and bolt action. On the left the bolt is removed for cleaning. It can be seen on the camp bed, together with a bayonet and a fighting knife.

Rifle, U.S. Springfield ·30, ·06 1903 Rifle, A1, A3, A4

Calibre: ·30, ·06, M1 and M2 cartridge.
Magazine: Staggered box type in receiver, capacity 5 cartridges.
Cartridge clips: Hold five cartridges.
Muzzle velocity: 2,700 ft/sec. (approx.), 2,800 with M2 ammunition.
Striking energy: 2,680 ft lbf approx.
Barrel length: 24 in.
Overall length: 3 ft 7¼ in. With new M7 bayonet + 10 in.
Weight of rifle: 8·69 lb, with bayonet about 9 lb 8 oz.
Effective range: Up to 600 yd.
Maximum range: 2,850 yd.

Rifle, U.S. Rifle ·30 M1 (Garand Semi-Automatic Rifle)

Calibre: ·30 U.S.
Magazine: Fixed box type in receiver loaded with clip.
Cartridge clip: Capacity 8 rounds. (This goes into the rifle with the rounds).
Ballistics standard for cartridges employed.
Barrel length: 2 ft.
Overall length: 3 ft 7 in.
Weight: 9 lb 8 oz plus 1 lb with bayonet M1905.
Range: Up to 1,200 yards with adjustable aperture sights.
Type of fire: Single shot, ie one shot for each pull of trigger.

See pictures on page 4, and page 70.

Setting up his exchange in a Normandy town, this Signal Corps telephone operator keeps his M1 Garand rifle ready for emergencies. He wears M1943 combat dress.

Carbine, U.S. ·30 M1 and M2, Carbine M1 A1 (Paratrooper's with folding stock)

Calibre:	*·30 U.S.*
Magazine:	*Box type detachable, 15 rounds capacity.*
Muzzle velocity:	*2,000 ft/s.*
Weight of bullet:	*110 grains, lead with metal jacket.*
Striking energy:	*Approx. 900 ft lbf.*
Barrel length:	*18 in.*
Overall length:	*35½ in.*
Weight:	*About 5½ lb with sling, oiler, and empty magazine.*
Accurate range:	*Appro·. 300 yd.*
Maximum range:	*Approx. 2,000 yd.*
Type of fire:	*Single shot, semi-automatic. ie, one shot per trigger pull.*

Submachine Gun, U.S. ·45 Thompson, M1928, and M1

Calibre:	*·45 M1911 cartridge, ball and tracer ammunition.*
Magazine:	*Type XX staggered box 20 and 30 shot capacity, type L drum 50 round. Type drum 100 round capacity (M1 only used box type).*
Muzzle velocity:	*950 ft/s.*
Striking energy:	*Approx. 440 ft lbf.*
Barrel length:	*10½ in. (With compensator 12½ in.)*
Overall length:	*With stock and compensator 33 in.*
Overall length:	*Without stock (M1938 only) 25¼ in.*
Weight:	*Without magazine 9 lb 13 oz.*
Weight:	*Loaded 20 round magazine approx. 1¼ lb.*
Weight:	*Loaded 50 round magazine approx. 4¾ lb.*
Accurate range:	*Approx. 300 yd.*
Cyclic rate of fire:	*600-700 rounds per minute.*

Here a U.S. soldier armed with the M1 carbine wears his overcoat and crouches behind a comrade in white camouflage clothing to demonstrate the contrast in visibility.

Firing the ·45 M3 sub-machine gun from the shoulder this soldier wears the fibre helmet liner while on a firing range exercise.

Front view of the BAR, here being fired without the optional bipod. The service issue anti-gas respirator is here seen in use. It was light khaki in colour.

Submachine Gun, U.S. Calibre ·45 M3

Calibre: ·45 M1911 cartridge, ball and tracer ammunition.
Magazine: Box type, capacity 30 cartridges.
Muzzle velocity: Approx. 920 ft/s.
Ballistics as for other submachine guns using this cartridge
Barrel length: 8 in.
Overall length: 29·8 in.—Stock extended.
22·8 in.—Stock folded.
Weight: Approx. 6 lb.
Range: Approx. 300 yards effective.

See picture on page 71.

Automatic Rifle, Calibre ·30 M1918, A1, A2 (BAR)

Calibre: ·30 M1906 or M1 cartridge.
Magazine: Detachable box type, capacity 20 rounds.
Muzzle velocity: Approx. 2,680 ft/s.
Weight of bullet: 150 grains, metal jacketed.
Barrel length: 24 in.
Overall length: 47 in.
Weight: Without magazine 15½ lb.
Weight: Loaded magazine 1 lb 7 oz.
Accurate range: Approx. 600 yd.
Cyclic rate of fire: About 500 rounds per minute.
Type of fire: Semi-automatic (one shot per trigger pull) —full auto.

This ·30 cal. Browning M1917A1 machine gun is being stripped for cleaning. The barrel has been withdrawn from the water-jacket and is being held by the man on the left, whilst other parts of the mechanism and the pistol grip lie on a cloth by his left knee. See also page 57.

Machine Gun, Calibre ·30 Browning M1917A1 (Water cooled)

Calibre:	*·30 M1 or M2 cartridge.*
Method of feed:	*Fabric belt holding 250 cartridges.*
Direction of feed:	*From left side of gun through to right.*
Muzzle velocity:	*M2 ammo, 2,800 ft/s.*
Weight of bullet:	*150 grains, full jacketed.*
Barrel length:	*24 in.*
Overall length:	*38 in.*
Weight of gun and pintle:	*33½ lb.*
Capacity of water jacket:	*7 pints (adds 7¼ lb to weight of gun).*
Weight of tripod:	*M1917—52⅓ lb. M1917A1—57 lb.*
Weight of belt and carrying chest:	*19 lb. belt and ammo alone 14 lb.*
Effective range:	*2,500 yd.*
Maximum range:	*About 4,000 yards.*
Rate of fire:	*400-500 rounds per minute. Type: full auto.*

Machine Gun, Calibre ·30 Browning M1919A6 (Air cooled light)

Calibre:	*·30 M1 or M2 cartridge.*
Other details as for M1917 A1	*except for:*
Weight:	*49·75 lb on small tripod.*
Range:	*3,500 yd.*
Maximum rate of fire:	*400-500 rounds per minute.*
Type of fire:	*Full auto.*
See picture on page 74.	

Here a ·50 calibre Browning machine gun M2 is in action at Huningen on the banks of the Rhine in December 1944. It is on a tripod ground mount, but was more familiarly seen pintle-mounted on AFVs and vehicles.

Machine Gun, U.S. Browning ·50 M2

Calibre:	** ·50*
Feed:	*Belt fed with 110, or 100 round belts (Metallic links)*
Muzzle velocity:	*2,400 ft/s to 2,600 ft/s.*
Barrel length:	*36 in. or 45 in.*
Overall length:	*(of Gun) 65 in.*
Weight:	*54 lb without barrel.*
Barrel weight:	*Approx. 25 lb for 36 in. and 30 lb for 45 in.*
Weight of loaded belt:	*Approx. 31 lb (100 rounds) + 4½ lb (chest).*
Maximum range:	*Approx. 7,200 yd.*
Type of fire:	*Full auto only.*

Produced with 3 types of barrel—Aircraft, Water-cooled, * ground type.

The ·30 calibre Browning machine gun M1919A6, complete with ammo box and tripod. This is the air cooled version of the gun which was a great deal lighter than the M1917A1 model.

The soldier in the foreground is aiming his ·30 calibre M1 carbine during a demonstration, whilst the M1 Rocket Launcher (bazooka) team prepare to fire. Note that as headgear all three men are wearing only the fibre liner parts of their helmets.

Rocket Launcher, Anti-Tank, M1 and M9 2·36 in. (Bazooka).

Projectile:	*Rocket.*
Length of launcher:	*55 in.*
Weight:	*14½ lb.*
Range:	*Up to 400 yards or 600 yards M9.*

57 mm Recoilless Rifle, M18

Weight:	*45 lb.*
Weight:	*With tripod 98 lb.*
Weight of projectile:	*2¾ lb.*
Range:	*4,300 yd.*
Rate of fire:	*15 per minute maximum.*
Crew:	*Normally 2, but could be used by one man.*

75 mm Recoilless Rifle, M20 (to be fired from ·30 Browning m/c gun tripod)

Weight:	*115 lb.*
Weight:	*With tripod 168 lb.*
Weight of projectile:	*14 lb.*
Range:	*7,200 yd.*
Crew:	*5 men.*

Mortar 60 mm, M19

Weight:	*45·2 lb.*
Weight of projectile:	*3-4 lb.*
Range:	*200-1,985 yd.*
Rate of fire:	*30-35 rounds per minute.*

Mortar 81 mm, M1

Weight:	*136½ lb.*
Weight of projectile:	*7-13 lb.*
Range:	*3,290 yd.*
Rate of fire:	*30-35 rounds per minute.*

A 60 mm mortar in action with its two man crew.

An 81 mm mortar in action in the Philippines in December 1944. Note the field telephone operator receiving ranging instructions on the left, whilst on the right can be seen bombs ready for firing.

Mortar 105 mm, T13 and T12 (Mounting)

Weight:	*Fully assembled 190½ lb.*
Weight of projectile:	*26 lb.*
Length:	*74 in.*
Range:	*2,000 yd.*

A 105 mm (4·2 in.) mortar fires from a position in Simmerath, Germany, in February 1945. Ammunition can be seen stacked in the foreground.

Mortar 155 mm, T25

Weight:	*600 lb fully assembled.*
Weight of projectile:	*60 lb.*
Length:	*72 in.*
Range:	*2,500 yd.*

U.S. infantry attacking in Normandy in July 1944. The soldier in the foreground is preparing to fire a grenade from his rifle. Censor has deleted sleeve badges. Man on right carries the M1 Rocket Launcher.

View of a 105 mm mortar in action, this time on the Italian front in January 1944.

Grenade

Weight:	*1¼ lb.*
Effective killing radius:	*10 yd.*
Range:	*By hand 35 yd. By rifle projector 225 yd.*

Rifle Grenade

Weight:	*1¾ lb.*
Range:	*365 yd.*
Killing radius:	*10 yd.*

See picture on page 77.

Flame Thrower

Weight:	*68-72 lb.*
Range:	*40 yd.*

A 37 mm anti-tank gun M3A1 firing on the Japanese in New Guinea. Note the pile of empty shell cases.

A flame thrower in action on the island of New Georgia in the Pacific. This was typical of several different man-portable models. Note rifleman giving covering fire to the operator.

37 mm Anti-tank gun, M3A1

Weight:	*(Gun only) 191 lb.*
Weight complete:	*900 lb.*
Overall length of gun:	*82½ in.*
Muzzle velocity:	*2,900 ft/s.*
Rate of fire:	*25 rounds per minute.*
Maximum range:	*12,850 yd.*
Ammunition:	*AP, HE, Canister.*

Towed by half-track, Jeep or 1 ton truck.

LEFT: Rear view of the 2·36 in. M1 Rocket Launcher shows the rocket about to be inserted into the launcher tube. The men are in twill summer combat dress wearing anti-gas respirators. Note the haversacks for these.

ABOVE: An infantry rifle squad in Normandy, July 1944. The nearest man (No. 2 on the BAR) carries an M1 carbine, the one in front of him has the BAR, and the rest have M1 Garand rifles.

Infantrymen inspecting a blockhouse in the Siegfried Line near Aachen in September 1944. They are armed with the ·30 calibre M1 Garand semi-automatic rifle. On the extreme right can be seen a medical corpsman. Third right is a rifleman in the top half of a camouflage suit.